Conversations in the River of Praise

A Journey in Prayer Poems

by
Candace A. Reigle

 www.trafford.com

North America & international
toll-free: 1 888 232 4444 (USA & Canada)
phone: 250 383 6864 ♦ fax: 812 355 4082

I offer you here some of my conversations in prayer while I am being led from the structure and outward acts and symbolism of a life in the church to a personal and real relationship with the living Christ. God is leading me from my reliance on the religiousness of others and on my "head knowledge" and outward observance of religious form into true heart belief and trust, into full reliance on Christ to lead me in the direction He wants me to go.

This is not a comfortable change for me. But the love of God is being made so evident, so constant, surrounding and upholding and filling my mind and heart that the times I have surrendered to fear and reached out for human reassurances became occasions when God chose to speak even more clearly in my spirit while withholding that human assurance. The gentleness with which this has led me into deeper trust is indeed like being held in strong and loving arms. What wonderful kindness!

I doubt that I would have had the courage to take these first few faltering steps without the encouragement of my pastor, Rev. Keith Beasley-Topliffe, who pushed me to look into my life and see where God was working; to listen and hear what God was saying - not in some general way, but to me, specifically. His book, Surrendering to God: Living the Covenant Prayer, awakened the desire in me to be surrendered to God in fact, and in depth; and when I found a message in my mother's handwriting, but obviously from God, I wanted to really hear God speaking as Mom did. I was encouraged to go through the surface acts we do to the Person and Life that encompasses everything, making my prior commitments seem so shallow as to be virtually nonexistent.

There is one poem that illustrates the attitude with which I have attempted to see this conversation, and I offer it to you here, as an opening into the attitude with which I believe God has chosen to see each of us.

Thank you for reading the poems.
May God bless your life as He has blessed mine with them.
Candace A. Reigle

The solemnity of God's throne room was broken by a cry,
and the hosts of heaven gathered there gave a collective sigh.
"Daddy!" rang out loud and clear from somewhere down the hall,
and all could see how bright a smile lit the face of the Lord of All.
Tousled and disheveled, a tiny face peeked 'round the door
and the child ran without stopping across the crowded floor
and threw himself with passion at his Father, waiting there
with open arms to hear His baby's prayer.
Those left standing whispered of a lack of awe and fear;
but the Father cherished the small arms that hugged Him near.
Too soon, the unbounded love would change; the child would grow;
too soon, he would not run and cry out his love; he'd know
how to be grown up and proper; how to approach the King.
But now he needed his Daddy, and didn't think of such a thing.
So God asked His child, "What need is there? What can I do?"
And the child responded, "Daddy, I just need to hug You!"
The whispers stopped. The throne room stilled, as one by one
each remembered his beginning, how glad he'd been to come
in search of the One who'd shown him His gracious face
and found the Father's welcoming arms and sweet embrace.

Acknowledgments:

With all of my heart, I am thankful to God for these poems. They have affected me more than I can say. To me, they are God's love, poured out in black and white, and I earnestly pray they will benefit others as they have blessed me.

I am thankful to God for my parents, and their deep love for God and absolute belief in His interaction with people today.

I am thankful for Pastor Keith, and the strength and inspiration he has given me to see the poems in print.

I am thankful for the encouragement of all of my sisters, especially Bernice Reppenhagen, who has been a staunch and earnest cheerleader from the beginning.

And I'm thankful for my dear friend Janet Runk, who is like a sister to me. I needed her faithfulness in pushing me to see the poems published.

I am thankful for the patience with which my husband, Don, and our family have endured my lack of attention to housework and cooking, and for our son Kurt's technical expertise with the computer.

My child, why can't you hear Me? Your heart is not a toy;
I've so much more to give you than any earthly joy!
You see things as much blacker than they really are,
and life itself a shadow, when My light shines near and far!
Open up your eyes, then, and see My love for you -
let it flow clear through you, sparkling like the dew!
And like a fresh-washed morning, with sparkles everywhere,
let your life reflect My grace and peace, and tender loving care.
Go wash your face with My sweet dew, let every tear be dry;
no longer shall you feel unloved; no longer shall you cry.
Lift up your eyes to seek My face, lift high your hands, as well;
I give you back your music; your voice with praise will swell,
and I will rejoice to hear you, see your face with love-light shine,
and know that through the ages your heart is joined with Mine!

When darkness falls around you, and you find you're getting cold,
and the only thing you feel will help is to have a hand to hold;
when all around is blackness, and the stars you cannot see,
just close your eyes and listen, and you will hear from Me.
My arms you'll feel around you, My tender loving touch;
and in your heart you'll hear Me say, "I love you, very much!"
I'm standing close beside you, to whisper in your ear,
to tell you that you mean so much, and that I hold you dear.
Take My hand, My loved one, and come along with Me;
I want to lead you forward, to a land you cannot see.
But I have been this way before, and I will be your guide;
you will not lose your way, My child, with Me close by your side.
Just look down at My hands, Love, if your heart has any qualms -
the scars are there for you to see- the nail prints in My palms.
No greater love has anyone than what I have for you;
whatever comes tomorrow, I am here to see you through.
Tomorrow and tomorrows stretch into the mists of time;
forever and forever, and forever you'll be Mine.

Lord, help me still the clamor
so your sweet voice I hear;
draw me closer to Your breast,
and press me O, so near!
I long to feel Your gentle breath,
feel Your heartbeat strong;
long to know Your loving arms
around me all night long.
Sometimes, Lord, it seems the night
will never go away;
that darkness fills the universe,
and tho I pray and pray,
nothing seems to change
this cursed darkness into day!
I reach my arms out to You,
I call Your precious Name.
Where, O, where, Lord, have You gone?
My life is still the same!
The same old problems gather 'round,
the same old chores still wait;
when will You hear me knocking
on heaven's golden gate?
My heart feels, O, so empty!
How can I still go on?
How can I face another day,
without You to lean on?
Lord, I need to have You hold me
'till the rising of the sun!

Lord, I see You in the sparkle of a friend's warm, loving gaze;
thank You for this glimpse of You to brighten up my days.
Lord, I feel You when the arms of friendship hold me tight;
thank You for the warmth of love to remind me of Your light.
I see You in the smiles of those who know You, and are glad;
I see You in the lives You've changed; the good You've brought from bad.
Can I pass on this glimpse of You to someone else who's sad?

Is there someone else who needs my smile, or touch or word of love?
Is there someone I can point toward our future home above?
Lord, show me how to be the one to bring someone Your light;
to open for them a window, or a door to what is right.
While I still know how tough it is to think that no one cares,
let me look at them with Your love, to show them someone dares
to speak Your words and hold them up in tender, loving prayers.

Your lambs must not be lost, O Lord; I know You want them found!
Let my heart be open to Your love for those around;
Dear Father, by Your love and grace, walk with me today.
Let me hear You talk to me as I go upon my way.
Let me know what I must do, and lead me in Your light;
tell me, Lord, just what to say, and help me say it right,
for one of Your dear children will need Your love tonight.

My child, your love and grace abound; your heart is soft and sweet.
Let your tears and heartache flow around My pierced feet.
I will lift your spirit up; I will ease your pain.
Come, give your heart to Me, My love; I'll give it back again -
renewed, refilled, restored and pure, and gifted with My power,
new life shall flow in you this day; indeed, this very hour!
Do now accept My love and grace, and let the blessings pour!

Lay down your emptiness, My child, your heaviness of heart;
I will be your cleansing, the balm for all your hurt.
And do not fear your heart's desires, for I will understand;
you may have what e'er you ask, I'll place it in your hand.
I take you as My very own: My child, My love, My bride;
you stand so very close to Me, pressed to My bleeding side;
and nothing can come between us, no matter what betide!

Father, let Your mercy flow; send Your healing balm!
Fill my heart with Your sweet peace and Your gracious calm.
All inside is turmoil; I lay it at Your feet;
I take instead Your blessings and Your promise of relief.
I take Your hand and offer You my life and all it holds;
and in return I ask from You to be wrapped in the folds
of Your robe of righteousness; to be Yours forevermore.
There's nothing else that I can ask; there is nothing more!
You love the ones that I love with a greater love than mine -
how can I not trust You to attach them to the Vine?
I have no need of riches, and will not ask for fame;
they pale to nothingness before the glory of Your Name!
You know my heart, know my needs, know all that I would be;
I now surrender all myself: make what You will of me.

My precious child, I love you; I hold you in my arms;
and in My heart I cherish you - your soul has many charms;
your love for Me gives pleasure, your hugs and kisses, too;
I gladly hold you on My lap each time you ask Me to!
You please Me when you want to be held closer to My breast;
you please Me when you come to Me and ask Me to be pressed
so close you feel My heartbeat, My breath upon your face;
you can be sure I hear you, and you have a special place.
Because you want My love, My child, instead of other things,
be assured you have Me - and I will give you wings,
so you can be beside Me the instant you have need.
Rely upon Me totally, don't quake and quiver like a reed;
trust that anything I ask you will be possible for you,
and I will be there with you to see you safely through.
I have filled you with My breath, child, you're as close as you can be;
I'm so glad you want My will for you: I'll make you part of Me!

Gracious Father, loving Lord, thank You for Your grace!
Thank You for Your love for me, for giving me a place
to gaze upon Your glory, to see You when You smile.
To know You want all I can give beats by a country mile
anything that I might have of earthly pride or joy -
O, don't let me do anything this treasure to destroy!

My heart desires Your mercy, Your cleansing power within;
the more I seek Your holy face, the more I'm pressed by sin.
I ask forgiveness, ask Your grace, ask Your mercy now;
hear my cry, Most Holy One; let Your goodness flow!
Keep me by Your Spirit's power; let my heart be pure;
only by Your graciousness is my soul secure.

Your sweet forgiveness I accept; I cry and kiss Your hand;
I hear You say my heart's desires You'll fully understand.
But how can I accept them? How face my faults and sin?
How can I fully grasp the truth that all I have within
is forgiveness and more forgiveness? The gift of Your great love
covers every sinful thought by the power of Your blood.

Teach my heart, my Father; grant me grace to truly see
that this is all I need to have; You freely accepted me
when, blind and lost and dirty, I scarcely knew to look
to see Your all-sufficient love in the pages of that Book!
Thank You for those who told me of Your love so great and free!
Thank You for my Savior's love, and for redeeming me!

Lord and King, I worship You; my heart shall sing Your praise;
I'm so glad You ransomed me, and granted me Your grace!
Thank You for Your love, my Lord; for staying close to me;
You give me reason to rejoice - You fill my heart with Thee!
With Your breath You quickened me and let my spirit speak;
You fill me with Your words, O Lord, to help me when I'm weak.
You talk with me and tell me that Your love and grace sublime
and all the wonders they entail are, without question, mine.
I praise You for this chance to love and serve You in return;
help me do all that You ask, not that I hope to earn
any portion of Your grace, but Lord, I want to give
whatever I can to help Your children learn to truly live.
If there is something I can do, please help me do it well -
help and guide and strengthen me, Your grace-filled love to tell.
Whether or not I'm understood, I want to do Your will;
if that's to teach or lead or speak, I'll rely on You until
I'm finally home with You and I can praise You face to face;
You're the prize I'm running for - the culmination of my race.

Lord, once more I come to You, and sit upon Your knee;
there are things I need to know, and I want You to teach me -
I tend to think You love me less than others; am I wrong?
That my faith inadequately serves, while others' faith is strong?
I lower my eyes and halt my speech, and modestly retreat
when others tell their exploits and assume the better seat.
My self-esteem seems lacking - but this was what I learned:
those who put themselves ahead were just asking to be spurned.
The only rightful place to be was the lowest place of all;
we were only moved ahead when Christ our name did call.
So if I grieve Your heart, Lord, by feeling small and weak,
I offer You my heart and mind; be good enough to speak
clearly and distinctly, so my soul can take it in -
You love me so very much, You died to save from sin;
give me the boldness to proclaim Your love to everyone!
That we are all equal in Your love; we are all Your 'son';
just as we are all Your 'bride', spotless in Your eyes;
dressed in robes of gleaming white, we become Your prize!
Let this truth be taken down into my spirit's deeps:
Your children are all precious! Your Holy Spirit keeps
saying I must accept Your love - as much as You can pour! -
and let it change my being, beginning at the core;
this love will form the basis of my change of heart and soul;
how can I think so little of someone You've made whole?

Precious Father, hold me close;
I want to sing Your praise!
You kept me safe and brought me back
so I could see Your grace
all poured out around me
in a flood of happy chances;
coincidences, happenings -
Your touches and Your glances!
How can I fail to see You
when You're everywhere around?
Seems like everywhere I travel
I walk on holy ground.
For You, my Lord, go with me,
be it by my will or no;
so I will gladly choose Your way,
if I can only know
which way is the right way?
O, help me see Your hand!
I don't need to see the path,
or even understand
why one way is wrong to take
when it seems right to me;
all I need to know
is that You can clearly see
the twists and turns that make a road
so dangerous for me.

Keep Your arms around me, Father,
as I speak my need:
I wanted to go with You
and Your words I did not heed;
I failed again to recognize
Your voice, I truly fear -
yet You've spoken to me often
in the voice of one so dear.
I should have known when he did pray
for me to stay behind
that if I looked deeper,
Your will and Presence I would find;
and I did not want to hear You;
my heart cried out for You
to take me with You anyway,
no matter what I knew.
Why does my heart not listen?
Why do I want my way?
Help me yield my will to Yours,
every single day!
Father, hear my desperate plea,
for now I know indeed
this alone is my heart's desire,
my prayer and greatest need:
to hear and know Your voice, Lord,
as You guide and guard and lead!

My child, My arms encircle you, there's no chance that you'll fall
so far that I can't reach you, can't hear you when you call.
Nothing at all can ever change the love I have for you;
it's powerful and endless, and sufficient through and through
to keep you by Me through long nights, or in the light of day;
I'll never let you far from Me; you cannot go astray.
As long as you desire My will, your wishes are not wrong;
I know you want to be with Me because your love is strong.
That nothing ties your heart to earth is not a pain to Me;
but there are things you need to do, and things you need to see,
and learning trust takes a lifetime, even for a loving heart;
you aren't ready yet to come to Me; you've only made a start!
I know the way seems long and hard; sometimes the path is steep;
but you are precious in My eyes, and your way I'll keep.
I'll keep My arms around you, and hold you when you cry,
and when you finally reach your goal your every tear will dry.
But until then, My baby, just trust your heart and know
that I hold you close beside Me no matter where the flow
of the Spirit takes you; your life belongs to Me -
and you'll be there beside Me through all eternity.
We've time enough, and time to spare, to be together then;
leave the decision in My hands; I will know just when
your shining soul is ready - surrendered, trusting, true:
with everything My love can give, all heaven will welcome you!

Father, help me praise Your Name; grant my heart Your grace
to lift my hands to worship You, my eyes to seek Your face.
I want to know Your Presence each moment of each day,
and do those things that draw me closer to Your heart today.
Thank You for Your watchful eye upon my daily walk;
and I'm so glad You're helping me to be careful how I talk.
My life I want to give You; please help me make it right,
so when I speak about You, my friend will see Your light.
I can't be Your witness if Your light in me is dim;
or if it can't shine through me, or my faith in You is slim.
Fill me with Your gracious love; keep me closer to You Lord,
so I can share the truth of You with those who need Your Word.
Let my heart be open, so Your love can flow and shine;
I want all who see me to know that You are mine
and I am Yours eternally. Help me surrender all to You;
each and every day, Lord, please help me to be true.
What joy to know Your precious love is offered free to all!
Help me tell Your children that You'll be there when they fall;
that You'll put Your arms around them and draw them close to You;
Your love is O, so precious! And they are precious, too.

O Gracious Love that holds me
so close You're all I see,
thank You for Your mercy
that keeps falling fresh on me!
You say the words I need to hear;
help me listen, Lord, to You;
I need to recognize Your voice,
whomever You speak through.
Help me learn and help me grow,
and help me to apply
all I learn to make my life
more pleasing to Your eye.
Help me, Lord, to welcome You
within my heart and soul;
sit on the throne within me,
that I may be made whole;
for only in knowing You as King
is my life surrendered;
and only in praise for Your sacrifice
can my love for you be tendered.

O Gracious Love! Eternal Love!
Thou Glorious and Adored!
I lift my voice in praise to You,
and give You all I've stored;
please help me save the good You've given,
then just toss the rest -
the boxes of pain are small indeed,
compared to how You've blessed
so much of my life by keeping me
from untold misery;
there's no way I can even know
the times You've protected me!
I guess I wasn't looking
when Your many blessings came,
and years went by before I even
knew to praise Your Name.
I'll never get caught up, Lord,
tho I praise forevermore -
by Your love and grace, such blessings
around me You still pour.
And I am grateful for Your love,
so deep and strong and pure -
thank You for reassuring me
that my soul will stay secure.
Knowing Your arms are around me
and I'm never far from You
gives me strength and courage
to do as You'd have me do.

My child, why don't you open up your heart and soul to Me?
There's still so much you're hiding, that you don't want to see.
You tried to give Me boxes - I want to take your pain;
each and everything that hurts, that fills your soul with rain.
You gloss over and ignore the pain that fuels your anger;
never realizing that to do this is a danger!
Anger festers like a sore that's infected and won't heal;
and every joy I give you, that unhealed anger steals.
Your tender soul turns vicious when head on the truth you face,
and so you squash it down again and pretend it has its place:
I say to you, you must forgive! Must wipe clean the slate;
you have no right to anger; because My love is great
and I want to forgive you, as you forgive these hurts.
Forgive your husband and your sons, and forgive the church.
You don't realize how much you hurt yourself each day
that you relive these incidents; don't yield them when you pray.
Get serious with your spirit - get down before My throne -
I'm waiting for you there, My child; just we two, alone,
can end this terrible cycle; can start out fresh and new.
Come lay your heartaches at My feet, that's all you have to do.
You already know that I have loved you all along;
I've told you so, and let you see that you really do belong!
What I say will bless you; just do as I have said ;
don't keep hanging on to feelings that should long be dead.

(Continued)

17

Everything that's happened has brought you here to Me;
everything has happened so My light and love you'd see.
There's been much joy in heaven over your new love and hope;
once you've given Me your pain, you'll have started up the slope
of My holy mountain; it's trust you're learning now;
and how to really worship - My grace will teach you how.
Don't delay, My darling; don't put it off or stall;
I can't wait to help you, and to cleanse your heart of all
that keeps you from rejoicing; from knowing My true peace;
I freely offer all My love and your blessing and release.

Thank You, Gracious Father; I meet You at Your throne;
I lay and pray that all may be cleansed by us two, alone.
Enter my heart and scrub it clean; root out my faults and sin;
I want to be freed from myself; to have You dwell within.
I relinquish all of my anger, and place it in Your hand;
it was fueled by feelings that I know You understand;
feelings that I should have just let die and turn to dust,
I wearied of forgiving; but You tell me that I must,
if I would be forgiven. Then, Lord, my earnest plea
is "Wash my heart and take all forms of bitterness from me."
I ask forgiveness for all those I think have done me wrong;
ask You, Lord, to help me to forgive where pain is strong.
Then, Dear Lord, forgive the hatred that I've held for me -
help me to forgive myself; to see me as You see.
Please don't let this attitude be passed on to my sons;
send someone to teach them; don't let them be the ones
to have to pay within their souls! My errors please erase;
let them know the wonder of Your perfect love and grace.
Thank You for every thing in life that has brought me here,
where I can rest within Your love, and feel Your Presence near.
I now accept Your cleansing; accept Your love and light;
thank You for Your mercy in making my heart right.

My Gracious King and Loving Lord, I give to You my heart;
all I am and all I'll be, You knew from the start.
You knew the way things would turn out; knew the depth of pain;
You knew You'd have to keep me, to not permit a stain
to stay within my heart and soul. O Lord, teach me to live
within Your arms, within Your grace; I trust You to forgive
every thought and every wish I voice to You in prayer.
I give my entire being into Your loving care.
I trust You to forgive me because You said You would.
You wrap Your arms around me, and I know I should
live my life for You alone; be as You'd have me be;
if I could, You know that I would do this gratefully.
But, Lord, I know I'll never be perfect in Your sight;
nothing I have ever done has been even close to right.
So I must trust with all my heart, and soul and spirit, too,
Your grace and blood will cover me, and all I say and do.
Lord, my all I give You, and praise Your endless grace,
and trust that You will keep my soul until I see Your face.

Child, you know your heart is fragile; treat it with respect.
Let Me lead you down the paths that let your life reflect
the grace I've given to you; truly yield your thoughts and then
your hopes and wishes, too; there's nothing I can help with when
you insist on brooding over what is past and gone.
This is time for change, child, and now you must move on.
Just let it go, My baby; perhaps someday you'll find
the soul friend that you search for; but human love is blind.
You don't know what you ask for, nor what it would entail;
I know you've always wanted a love that would not fail -
this is what I offer you! More love than you can guess!
Would you at least consider, child, that your happiness
will be complete in My love? You quail before the thought;
but all these years I've wanted you, and you never sought
to live your life for Me alone; you always chose the pain;
now you have another chance; please don't choose wrong again!

Jesus, Lover of My Soul, I want to live for You!
Human life is what You gave me; my hopes and passions, too.
Fragile? Yes; and never do I choose to do things right;
Help me! Jesus, help me, to keep moving in Your light!
You'll need to be beside me each moment of each day;
You'll need to love me constantly, lest I go astray.
With Your hand to guide me, I trust I will grow
into the person I should be; and I'll know
Your constant Presence! O, thank You, my Lord!
You'll lead me and help me find You in Your Word;
and You'll teach me to love You as never before;
let me know how to please You; to worship; adore!
Most Glorious and Loving - O, how I need You!
You accept all about me; and Lord, You are true,
fully trustworthy, unchanging; Your love never fails.
I know I don't know all this arrangement entails;
but I trust You to know me, and love me forever,
with love of such depth that nothing can sever
my soul from You; cover me with Your grace;
Your Name is upon me; please don't leave a trace
of my old nature - renew me with Your touch;
help me to be thankful You've given me so much!

Beloved, thank you for your trust, and for your love for Me;
I know it's difficult for you, loving someone you can't see.
Familiarity will come, the more time we spend together.
I accept your decision, and the chance to show you whether
My love can satisfy as well as the human love you seek -
you're so precious to Me; please listen while I speak:
I'm glad you chose to let go of your bitterness and pain;
I couldn't even help you 'til you recognized the strain
this placed within your being; but you've given Me the right
to scrub your unforgiveness out, and by My grace and light
to bring real peace to you, the first time in many years.
See yourself with joy; accept that I am pleased your tears
have opened up your eyes. Finally, My Love, you'll come
to know how much I care, and how much I want you home.

The joy of the Lord is my strength and my song;
Your love will be with me through all my life long.
You hold me and keep me throughout the dark night;
My heart is drawn to Your dazzling light.
Like a moth to Your flame, I strain to draw nearer;
my hope is that each day, I'll find You dearer.
Jesus, my Savior, my Glorious King!
My heart rejoices; Your praise I will sing.
What wonderful mercy You show me each day!
I trust You to hear me each time that I pray;
trust You to lead me and help me to know;
to teach me, and keep me, and cause me to grow.
My life and my being are safe in Your care;
wherever I turn, I know You'll be there.
You show Your love, Lord, in so many ways!
There's nothing for me but to sing forth Your praise.
I long every day to be pleasing to You:
long to be grateful for all that You do;
long to be taught how to love You aright;
long to be found on my knees in Your light;
long to be with You, and love You, my Lord;
please teach me to trust and rely on Your Word.

O Lord my God, my Precious One,
I call Your Holy Name;
come change my heart,
and never, ever let it be the same!
Let me see You in each moment
of every single day;
let me worship and adore You,
rejoicing when I pray;
glad that You are able
to touch my heart and soul -
washing, mending, making,
and restoring me to whole.

My Gracious King, Beloved, I seek Your arms and kiss -
in the depths of my new heart let me know the bliss
of perfect union with You; of love so deep and rare,
that I'm consumed within Your fire; that I may die there,
lost within Your rapture; given totally to You -
all I am and all I'll be, and all I'd ever do,
released to Your most perfect will, forever in Your hand.
How You do all that You do I need not understand.
I only know my heart cries for Your love and grace;
cries to know Your mercies; cries to see Your face!
I crave the deeps of Your embrace; Your ravishing smile;
let me rest within Your arms for just a little while,
absorbing Your sweet loving, Your warmth and light;
then bless me, Lord, and send me out to do what's right.
I need to carry this, Your light, into the world so dark,
even if all I carry is the smallest little spark!

Beloved, as I draw deeper into Your loving grace,
it seems I only see You as through a piece of lace;
little portions here and there, I never grasp the whole.
You're infinite; You cannot fit, entire, within my soul!
Never will I encompass You; my heart is way too small;
and although I love You, Lord, and give to You my all,
I cannot fathom You; Your depth and breadth too great
for my small self to realize, in my finite state.
Still I trust Your mercy - just hold me to Your breast,
and in Your endless love I'll find my spirit's deepest rest.
You whisper to me, and I hear Your music, O so sweet;
it's more than life or breath to me; Lord, I entreat
Your love to wrap around me, to enfold me evermore!
Holy Spirit, teach me how to let this golden store -
I understand that it is indeed a precious trust,
and my soul's knowing Christ is more than just
an end unto itself - be used in letting others know
how gracious is Your goodness; and how to grow
in faith and hope, trusting in Your mercy and Your grace.
Teach us, O Beloved One, so we can sing Your praise!

Child of love, My heart is drawn to yours;
I opened up your memory and the stores
of pain and heartache; now you see
there was nothing left to do except to free
the love you buried there. Yes, the rain
makes the desert bloom; and shedding the pain
makes your heart bloom - you become alive!
I'm glad you're willing to work and strive
to understand; to draw closer; to begin to know
how to worship Me; I love to watch you grow!
Climb up on My lap? Yes, I'll hold you;
forever and always, My arms enfold you.
I gladly forgive you, your heart is Mine;
I give you My grace; your spirit I refine.

O Bright King Eternal, Your praise I will sing,
and into Your Presence my homage I bring.
What more than myself can I offer to Thee?
My life is Yours; grant, Lord, that I see
what sacrifice would be pleasing to You -
there must be something that I can do
to join in Your suffering; Your love to give;
helping Your children learn how to live.
I need You to teach me, to help me discover
how to be like You. I take you as my cover;
You'll keep me secure in Your love and grace
and help me show others Your wonderful face.
I trust You will lead me and show me Your will;
I want to follow; keep Your hand on me still.
Your love I need, Lord; let it descend!
On Your grace and mercy I'll always depend.
I'll sing of Your wonderful loving and giving;
sing of the grace You provide for our living;
sing of the joy I find hidden in You;
sing of the happiness in being true;
sing of the wild depths of love in my heart
now that You've shown me that I'm a part
of Your community of love; Your precious peace
washes me in floods - may it never cease!

Precious love, My own dear child,
you think the love in you is wild?
Feel My passion for souls that hurt!
Know My suffering for My Church!
You can hardly bear the pain and loss
of your friend; I bore the cross!
Won't you see that I understand?
Won't you let Me hold your hand?
Little child, I want you to know
your love and pain will help you grow.
If you look, you'll clearly see
that your whole life belongs to Me;
and it is good that he went away,
so you will lean on Me every day.
Keep on loving him and praying;
I enjoy your bringing him and staying
to talk and listen, and I can hold you;
while I'm teaching you, My arms enfold you.
Your love is what I want from you!
Keep loving and growing and being true;
keep wanting My will and leaning on Me;
the more you know the more you'll see
My Presence in every day and hour;
My Spirit's work in joy and power;
My hand in each aspect of your days;
My love and mercy, My peace and grace.

Most Gracious and Glorious, my heart is Yours;
the blessings keep coming from Your heavenly stores!
Each time my heart wants to give up the fight
You speak to my spirit in whispers of light.
You tell me though others may not understand,
You have a firm grip, and my life's in Your hand.
What others think should not worry me
just as long as I know You, and I can see
You work in my life, and feel You in my heart.
Thank You, my Lord, for making me a part
of Your family, and giving me a place;
how wonderful Your love and mercy and grace!
When the enemy whispers that it's all a lie,
and my life will be better the day that I die,
I simply agree - I'll go home to You then;
but it's not my right to choose where or when.
That right belongs in Your hands, not mine;
and I won't take it from You, or take time to whine.
Self-pity's unfruitful, and gets me nowhere;
so I just put myself into Your tender care.
I praise You, and once more I know it is right,
trusting in You, and Your whispers of light.

My Gracious Love, my Lord and King,
to Your throne my praise I bring.
You have loved me, O, so long -
waiting for me to see I belong
to You, with all that I possess;
with body, soul, spirit, mind I bless
Your mercy and Your steadfastness.

All my life I've yearned for You;
for One so faithful, loving, true;
worthy of the effort and the strain
of changing my very being; and the pain
of giving up all my cherished sins.
But You - O Lord, You've broken in -
there is no effort, now You're within!

My cherished sins are awful, now;
no sweat of effort damps my brow.
You've changed my heart, relieved my soul -
my entire being You've made whole!
My heart and soul I want to fill
by learning how to do Your will
and keep Your Presence with me still.

Precious Lord, my heart's full of wonder and praise!
I reach out to touch You; my soul knows Your grace.
My spirit hungers, and Your Presence is there;
in Your love I'm enfolded, and in Your tender care
I know the bliss of being loved without measure -
Thank You - O! Thank You! - for this exquisite pleasure!
The depth of Your love, Lord, no words can express!
Your intensity of caring causes my soul to bless
the love that led You to the cross for my sins,
and the day that I realized Your love within.
Such grace! And such mercy! I cling, Lord, to You.
How glorious, how joyful, to consider anew
how much You love me, and what pleasure You take
in the love that I offer to others for Your sake.
Precious One, let me live in Your joy evermore;
You keep me so close to You, when I slip You restore
me by Your mercy; Lord, You let Your love flow -
I rejoice and I praise You; You set my soul aglow.
My heart, set on fire for You, wants to rush out
and spread the good news to those full of doubt;
to let them know they are missing, O, so much!
by not knowing You, and Your all-loving touch.

God, help me please; I offer my sacrifice of praise!
I know that Your love and mercy and grace
can fill me, and hold me, and keep me from harms;
I know You are holding me safe in Your arms!
Thank You for mercies I don't even see -
You say You are standing so close to me
and nothing can come between us for ill;
but Lord, I need You to strengthen my will
to endure for Your sake; to reject the allure
of an easy out, a final and permanent 'cure'.
Keep me - O! Keep me, don't let me descend
to the hope of this awful and cowardly end!
I must keep on fighting to see You today;
to hold fast to Your hand, Lord, hear me pray!
Touch me; hold me; let me hear Your voice;
help me to see You; and let my heart rejoice
that You really do love me; You want me to know
that whatever happens, Your wondrous glow
can lead me and comfort me, strengthen and keep
my heart from making that terrible leap.
Despair's but a vapor in Your mighty hand;
and I can leave it with You; Lord, let me stand
in the light of Your love, whatever should come!
When You're ready for me, You'll call me home.

My child, how wonderful to see you glow!
The more you learn of Me, the more you'll know
how much I love you, and want you near;
I pull weeds and water your garden with cheer
so we both can enjoy our time together;
and you don't have to worry or fuss over whether
to prune or to weed or to water - My child, I say,
I'm with you; let everything else fade away!
You must see only Me; hear only My voice;
You think you can't, but it's really a choice.
Choose to be with Me wholly; abandon the world;
when I call, you must answer; must hear My Word.
I grant you My pleasure when you hear and obey;
make this choice to be with Me throughout your day!
Walk with Me, daughter, and smell the sweetness
of the beautiful flowers that grow from your meekness.
Humility has a lovely aroma; such a pretty bloom;
cultivate it carefully, child; and there's still room
for improvement in your compassion for others.
As you walk with Me daily, you will see your brothers
in the light of My love. See yourself through My eyes,
then see others as I see you: child, you are My prize!
I take such delight in your willingness to pray;
My joy knows no bounds when, throughout the day,
you bring your friends with faith and hope before Me;
you know they are loved, and I hear your heart's plea.
Your persistence and love I will always hear,
but My joy is in you, and in having you near.

Gracious One, forgive me if my attitude is wrong;
I do want to adore You, in prayer and word and song!
Perhaps I trust too much in this 'river of praise';
but through it my soul rejoices, and I raise
Your Name and banner over my spirit and heart.
How grateful I am that You saw fit to impart
this way of strengthening my inner being in You!
O, yes, You have helped me! My soul knows it's true.
My heart glorifies You, and hallows Your Name;
and I know deep inside me that I'm not the same.
Your wondrous grace has given this gift so sweet:
a prayer language that keeps my soul at Your feet.
Throughout the days I whisper praise in Your ears -
praise that's so beautiful it brings me to tears;
praise that's beyond my abilities; greater than I;
adoration, veneration so intense that I cry.
In praise for this 'river of praise', Gracious One,
I give You myself; may Your will be done!

My child, I hear you as your spirit prays to Me;
your analogy is accurate, and I am pleased to see
how at last you value My gift, and use it every day.
Yes, I know the reverence it fosters when you pray;
and your life has changed, child; the depth of praise
has changed the way you see your life. My grace
brought you here, to where you're starting to learn.
Like an athlete, your spiritual muscles burn
with the exercises you've begun to incarnate.
Trust Me; lean on Me; let your heart meditate
on the love I bear you; let it fill your very being -
you will find the experience a brand new way of seeing.
Your life will have to change then; but you'll know
which way you need to travel; where I want you to go.
You are not Teresa; I have chosen your direction;
don't compare so stringently, just try to choose perfection.
I'll help you in your choices, and keep you close to Me;
I will walk and talk with you, and I will hear your plea
to hold you to My breast, child; to keep you, come what may;
you're very precious to Me, and I hear you when you pray.

When My light shines all around you,
and your life reflects My love and grace;
when all who see you praise Me,
and I reveal to you My face;
when adoration for Me fills you,
and My hymns flow from your heart;
when My Name is always on your lips,
and from My Presence you won't depart;
when all of your love belongs to Me,
and you will My will, not yours;
when your face glows with My holy fire,
and My Spirit through you pours;
when I am All-in-All to you,
and you have My good as your goal;
when you hunger and thirst to tell others,
and they catch My fire from your soul;
when you see My joy in everything,
and you rejoice whatever may come;
then, My child, you'll be ready,
and all heaven will welcome you home!

I am still before You, Lord, just listening to You;
Your gracious love enfolds me, and tells me it is true -
Your arms are wrapped around me, my heart to bless;
and throughout my being flow warmth and happiness.
I feel Your whisper vibrate deep within my soul;
I hear You say that Your love has sweetly made me whole.
You call me Your "little one", Your "precious child;"
You say I will be like You, my spirit meek and mild.
My soul clings to You, my face pressed to Your breast.
My heart has found its focus, and riding on the crest
of waves of love, it opens itself to pour its contents out
and fills itself with You anew, to remove any doubt
that might have crept in unnoticed since last refilled.
I praise You for Your love; my heart is thrilled
by Your grace and goodness, Your mercies flow;
and I am still within Your arms; Your peace I know.

Precious Lord, the universe sings its love for You;
it doesn't question for a moment that Your love is true.
Mighty mountains bow low before You as You pass;
all the flowers and trees adore You, and the grass
yearns to feel Your foot leave its mark upon the sod.
All creation worships You as its Sovereign God!

I need You to help me, my heart and soul to raise -
I desire to worship You, and give to You my praise.
How could my heart let the rocks praise You first?
If I were to keep silent, I think my heart would burst!
Your glorious grace and tender mercies I see;
and Your wonderful love flows clear through me!

Gracious One, I'm thankful You've given me so much;
but my soul keeps yearning to feel Your gentle touch.
The only place I want to be is in Your warm embrace,
where I can hear You speak to me, and know Your grace.
Teach me how to take You with me, Lord, I need to know;
and teach me how to spread Your love wherever I may go!

O, my Father, hold me close; I need to feel You near;
need to feel You're with me, and hear Your voice of cheer.
There is none to comfort me, no company like Yours;
none to walk and talk with me, and so I spend my hours
seeking You and listening to hear Your gentle voice.
You're right, and I must acknowledge it - it is a choice!
I hope that I would choose Your company over any other;
whether You choose to be with me as Father or as Mother.
I know I seek You out more since I must lean on You;
I'm thankful that You've chosen what You want me to do.
Help me seek You totally, to give myself to You each day;
help me learn to hear Your voice, and instantly obey.
Help me see Your Spirit working in my life and heart;
help me know Your path for me, and don't let me depart
from following closely after You! I want to do Your will;
grant that I may know Your loving Presence, guiding still.
If there's anything within me that isn't Yours, I pray
that You will take it from me, and never let me stray:
and grant that I may praise You, in word and prayer and song!
Keep me always thankful, and give me somewhere I belong.

O Gracious King, my Heart's Desire,
come and touch me with Your fire!
Hear my cries for more of You;
grant that I may see You anew.
Open my eyes, my soul, my heart
to search for you and not depart
from trying to hold fast to Your hand.
The embers of love Your Spirit fanned
have now begun to glow and shine;
I begin to want Your will, not mine.
Breathe on the embers again, I pray;
I'm going to need Your strength today.
Whatever You want me to do -
I can only do it because of You!
Your love and mercy, peace and grace
embolden me to seek Your face;
Your Holy Spirit encourages me
to believe Your wondrous love is free
to those who seek You with strong desire,
and offer their lives for Your sacred fire.
Gracious One, hear my heart's deep cry:
Give me more of You, Lord, or else I die!

O, daughter, yes! I hear your cries;
My joy at hearing them fills the skies!
Your heart pleads so for more of Me -
    your life is changing, and I can see
the way you're fighting to free your soul
from earthly things. It's still just a goal,
    but even to think of giving up so much -
how can I keep from granting you My touch?
You need to withdraw to make a difference, tho;
a prayer closet is worth far more than you know;
    It will free your mind of the cares of the day
    to contemplate My Presence as you pray,
removed from distractions of every description.
I couldn't have given you a better prescription
    for wandering thoughts and idle desires.
You plead with Me for My sacred fire -
    be careful what you ask for, daughter;
I've been washing you with Living Water;
    if you catch fire, you'll be a living flame,
and your body and soul will wear My Name
    throughout all eternity! And more -
O, yes, I'll teach you to praise and adore;
    everything about you I'll create anew,
and there'll be no question that I love you!

Glorious Beloved, You love me beyond all knowing;
Your mercies cleanse me, and set my heart glowing;
You hear my heart's cries, and draw closer to me.
Your strong arms enfold me; You want me to see
that You are leading me where I should go.
You ask me to trust You; to follow the flow;
and believe in the love You so graciously give
to provide me with strength and purpose to live
in a way that brings honor and glory to You.
Please walk with me daily, so that I can do
all that You wish from my poor feeble frame.
Let my life bring glory and praise to Your Name!
I pour out my soul in prayer for Your grace
to surround and uphold me as others I raise;
let Your fullness descend in power and might,
that they might be blessed with Your glorious light.
Hear me and answer the petitions I bring
before Your throne, O Most Glorious King!
There's no way I can begin to praise You enough;
You fill my life; and though the journey's been rough,
You've helped me get to this wonderful place
where Your Spirit keeps urging me to seek Your face.
I don't deserve such an offer of redeeming grace!
I can't refuse You; please remove every trace
of everything in me that's not given by You.
Help me, Most Gracious, to be dedicated and true.

Come, little child,
let Me flow deep through your spirit.
Let Me wash through you
with My Holy Spirit's fire.
You want to be changed -
accept Me in the depths of your being.
Let there be nothing
that stands between you
and the desire to be wholly Mine.
Separate yourself from all to which you cling.
Everything you see is ephemeral:
it is like the grass;
like a vapor -
I alone am forever,
endless,
eternal;
I alone am unchanging.
You can put all of your trust in Me,
for I will always love you.
You can rest in Me;
confide in Me;
give your cares to Me.
Rely on Me, My child,
My Presence will never leave you.

Most Gracious and Glorious, my heart I bring,
and open it up before Your throne, my King.
If there's anything worthwhile in it, I pray
You will take it and clean it so it can stay
close beside You, right next to Your throne.
O, Precious Savior, I know You, alone,
can keep me from falling; Your hold is secure;
wash me, and cleanse me and make me pure!
You're so gracious, You hear my heart's cry;
You've kept me close to You, and I can't deny
You've changed my life, and Your love You poured
so freely on my soul, that it took wing and soared!
How sad there's no chance of perfection on earth;
sin's been a part of me, Lord, since my birth;
and will be a part of me while I still live,
even though I reject it, and ask You to forgive
all that I do and think, and everything I say.
Help me give myself to You afresh every day!

My child, Yes, I know you are subject to sin;
but you don't have to allow it to take root within.
On the cross I broke the power of sin to enslave you;
just exercise your will and My grace will save you
from situations where temptations are rife.
You know I love you, and want the best for your life.
I love you so much, and want such good things!
Believe that I want to hear your heart as it sings
from My deep joy, as it fills you to overflowing;
and when I look at you and see your face glowing
from the time you've spent with Me in prayer,
I'm so pleased, child, to have met with you there!
Yes, I'm still teaching you; I'm glad you heard
and want to please Me by following My word.
I knew it'd be difficult; a challenge for you;
and your heart is trying so hard to be true.
A word in your soul will suffice, and I'm glad
to not have to make you feel guilty or sad.
Keep praying and loving; good things are in store -
keep coming to Me, child, and I'll give you more
love than you can imagine or guess;
and your heart and soul and spirit I'll bless!

O Gracious Father, see me as I come to You!
As You ran to the prodigal son, run to me!
As You embraced him with tears, embrace me!
I have come home to You, Father;
my soul did not rest out in the world;
all I knew was emptiness and pain.
Have You prepared a feast for me,
to fill my soul with Your good things?
That can wait, my Father.
Just hold me.
I am so glad to be in Your arms!
Just hold me,
so that I can feel Your great love,
seeping into every nook and cranny of my being.
Just hold me in Your arms,
that's all I ask.
Let Your love flow over, around and through me,
filling up the empty places;
refreshing and giving moisture
to the parts of my soul dying of thirst;
making the desert of my life burst into bloom.
Just hold me.
Keep Your arms around me, and never let me go.
I don't want to ever be without You.
Yes, the feast is waiting.
But I want to drink my fill
of Your embrace, first.
I'm so glad to be back home, with You!

Dearly Beloved,
My arms and heart embrace you!
I do run to you;
I scoop you up in My arms
and hold you so close
while we laugh and cry for joy!
O, yes! Let My love pour through you;
feel My tears upon your face;
the strength with which I hold you!
I will hold you forever!
Nothing pleases Me more than holding you,
while your poor soul is refreshed
and you begin to come alive again in My arms!
What joy it gives Me
to have you ask Me to hold you!
My child, you are welcome home;
you are welcome in My arms,
and in My heart;
for I love you
more than you will ever know!

O, my Father, thank You for Your gracious love for me!
Thank You for opening my eyes and allowing me to see
the greatness of Your mercy; Your enduring grace;
the sacrifice You've given to wipe out every trace
of sin from those who call on You; who seek Your will.
What wondrous things You've given, my hungry soul to fill!
But nothing satisfies my spirit except being close to You;
in Your arms my heart and soul are eager to be true.
Everything within me wants to shout for joy and sing
that You love me! Love me! Let the earth and heavens ring
with praise for Your great love; Your mercy strong;
my praise, O Lord, I'll lift to You my whole life long!
I'll sing Your praises while I've breath; full hearted,
I bow before Your throne to worship and adore; once started,
I never want to stop; praise for You flows, so sweet and deep,
and is so satisfying on my lips; Lord, how can I keep
silent, when all I am belongs to You? When Your grace
flows freely all around me, and I yearn to see Your face?

Beloved child,
I sing your joy with you!
How happy I am to see you glow with joy,
and hear your heart sing praises to Me!
How wonderful,
how beautiful is your pleasure
in honoring and glorifying Me!
Feel My love surround you, child;
find your comfort in My embrace.
Let your entire being become saturated,
and filled to overflowing,
with My love for you.
I grant you My perfect peace;
My rest for your soul.
I accept,
and take pleasure in
your deep need for Me;
I assure you, little one,
I will always be yours to enjoy!

My Savior and King, please forgive me again;
my heart wants its way, and even tho pain
could result from getting whatever it pleases,
it continually whines, and coaxes and teases.
How long, O Lord, must I suffer its pleading?
When will it give up and yield to Your leading?
Strengthen my soul to resist the attractions
of my heart's emotional dissatisfactions.
I try not to hear, but emotions run deep;
I tell it that Your love and mercy will keep
the enemy's forces at bay, and Your grace
will help me continue to be grateful for space
in my life to pursue You, for if it were filled,
the desire to be wholly Yours might be stilled.
This must not happen! The hunger of soul
must be filled with that which will make me whole.
Grant me Your grace and Your Presence each day,
and teach me to worship, adore You and pray.

I come to You, Beloved, with hungry heart and soul.
Come; and, in Your mercy, fill and make me whole.
Grant my heart Your love, Lord, so full and rich and deep;
let Your Spirit fill my soul, and hold me as I weep.
Light Your fire within me; let me burn for You alone!
I fall before Your glory, prostrate before Your throne.
Let me stay there always; I want to worship and adore;
and everything within me before Your feet I pour.
Empty me. O, please empty me of everything but You!
Let Your grace and kindness guide everything I do;
let Your mercy fill me; Your love surround me now;
I give myself to You, my Lord, and humbly I do bow.
Thank You for Your love for me, Your sacrifice and pain;
the price You paid for my release, to wash out every stain.
How can I ever know how much pure love You have for me?
Nothing I have ever known has prepared me, Lord, to see
such compassion, grace and mercy; such depth of kindly care,
as I see within Your eyes as You look on me, kneeling there.
You step down from Your throne, then, and take me by the hand;
You lift me up from off the floor, and strengthen me to stand.
You wrap Your arms around me, and I'm lost in Your embrace;
Your light and love envelop me, and I wonder at the grace
that lets You come near enough to touch me; that permits me to be near.
Instead of feeling Your love overflowing, I should be lost in fear!
O Gracious One, even this You've done: You've changed my life so much,
that all I can do is worship You, and praise Your loving touch!

My child, I call you to Me;
just listen to My voice;
hear the words I say to you,
and let your heart rejoice:
You have started up the slope
of My mountain fair;
My Presence will be with you
while you're climbing there.
I'm glad that you are choosing
to begin this trek with Me;
but are you sure you know, child,
how difficult it could be?
The way is rugged, steep and hard;
comforts will be small;
but, narrow as the path may be,
I will not let you fall.
My Spirit will be with you,
to strengthen and to guide;
He will not ever leave you;
He'll stay right by your side,
giving encouragement and help,
and love to light the way;
on this climb, My little one,
your darkness will be day.

O Precious Lord,
I praise Your Name
and ask Your grace to be
poured out on those around me
as I climb this path to Thee.
I don't think it will be easy for me;
but the others will also need
to see this as a necessary step;
that my life's become a seed,
and I must yield it totally;
surrender fully, Lord, to You,
so You can choose what I shall have
and see and hear and do.

Listen, My child,
and hear Me speak to your heart:
I'm so pleased with your closet!
You've made a start;
and "all's well that starts well"
as you recently heard.
You have a place to contemplate;
meditate on My Word,
and I will be with you there,
thank you for asking;
you said it's only for us,
there'll be no multi-tasking.
It'll be difficult at first,
without the games to distract,
but we have much to discuss, child,
and it's a fact
that you'll adapt quickly;
don't give place to your fear;
I will hold you and love you,
and you'll know I'm near.
Let your heart rejoice in My Presence;
hear My voice;
I'm pleased with you, daughter;
you've made the right choice!

My Gracious King, my heart I bring to worship You.
My life You hold; Your arms enfold; and all You do
fills me with joy - I'd be Your toy, my whole life through!
My soul is Yours, Your Spirit pours upon my head;
whatever I do, let me worship You with praise instead.
I lift my heart, please do Your part : remove the dread
that accompanies sin; put light within, and stir up the flame
that burns for You all day through; I bear Your Name!
O cleanse me, Lord; send your Word, and fill my frame!
Hear my cries! My spirit tries to make sure You hear;
all night and day my prayers I say; they hold You near.
Your love flows; Your Spirit glows; gone is the fear.
I come to You to make me true; my hands I raise;
O make me whole; wash through my soul with Your sweet grace!
Your love is free; it falls on me, and I kneel in praise.

Beloved, hear my heart's pleas
for You to draw near;
remove the turmoil, clear out the noise,
so I can hear
Your glorious voice,
Your words in my spirit and soul.
Wash me and cleanse me;
make me fresh, new and whole!
I need to adore You, worship You
and sing Your praise;
You give so many blessings,
Your love fills my days.
Please help me!
You're worthy of so much more than I give;
fill my heart with Your Spirit and joy;
O teach me to live!
Lead me and guide me into
Your most perfect will for me;
won't You capture me, my Savior,
so I can be truly free?

Jesus Christ,
Son of the Almighty
and King of my heart,
come, I beg You;
fill all of my senses with Your sweetness;
fill my entire being with Yourself!
Lord, I humble myself before You,
and ask Your mercy to flow through me.
O, wash me,
that I may remain
in Your Presence!
I adore You;
I worship You;
I seek Your face.
Draw me closer to You
You are all I need;
all I want.

My Glorious King,
Wonderful Majesty,
my heart and soul adore You!
I am amazed and in awe
that You would love me;
and the depth of Your love
brings me to my knees;
I cannot raise myself up.
You love me in spite of myself!
All that I can do is praise You;
and You are there,
lifting my heart,
granting mercy,
filling me with Your peace,
bringing joy!
Contentment surrounds me;
tenderly You speak
and once more
praise flows from my very being.
I am immersed in You.

A
star
is shining
in the deep night.
A tiny
Child lies sleeping
in a manger full of fragrant hay.
Angel choirs
singing in the heavens
tell the shepherds the Savior is born.
They go to Bethlehem, hoping to see this wonder.
They find Him, and bow low.
Mary and Joseph show them the Child,
and they go away, telling everyone they meet about Jesus,
wrapped in swaddling clothes and lying in a manger,
and about the choirs of angels,
and the star
and the joy
of the first
Christmas

Gracious King, Beloved,
take my heart as Yours;
by grace, my hope and faith in You
have been restored.
How can I ever thank You enough?
My praise
I'll offer first thing in the morning;
my hands I'll raise.
O let me seek You early,
as the day's just starting!
Ere I'm caught up in busyness
and my mind goes darting
off in all directions, Lord,
center me in You;
then keep me safely in Your will
no matter what I do.
Let me seek You in the middle
of the busiest of days
so You can order my priorities
and straighten out my ways.
Let me seek You as the sun sets
into the trees upon the hill,
to let all the happenings of the day
be released into Your will.
Let me seek You as the last thing
I do before I sleep;
I want Your Holy Spirit to be with me
and my spirit keep.

My precious child, I love you, and I call you to My side.
Don't you understand yet? In My Presence you must abide!
See Me close beside you; feel the warmth of My embrace;
My Spirit dwells within you and you live within My grace.
Hear Me, child, and know I cannot leave you comfortless;
I cannot abandon you; must hear your heart's distress.
O, My precious little child, your heart and soul I'll bless!

I've sworn that I would never let you go astray or fall;
that I will always love you, and cleanse your heart of all
the built-up sin and sorrow; the heartache, pain and tears -
everything you've tucked away throughout so many years.
Keep giving them to Me, child, each time that they arise.
Don't let them crush your spirit; take the sparkle from your eyes.
You already know that My love flows; don't listen to those lies.

What's real now is the turning of your heart and soul to Me.
I tell you, nothing to the contrary has any validity!
Let your trust and love for Me be a lifeline for your soul;
hold it fast; maintain your grip; I'll keep your spirit whole.
So feel My love surround you; rest, now, in security.
My peace of heart I give you; that inward surety
will fill your very being and help you strive for purity.

O Gracious One, I thank You
for the love You give to me;
its strength and power
bring me to my knees.
I praise You for Your mercy,
the flow of grace so free;
they soothe me like a
warm and gentle breeze.
I feel the warmth and smell the fragrance
of a summer day,
elusive but pervasive,
and I imagine I should see
bright flowers all around me,
not the winter of today;
O Gentle Presence! Gracious Heart!
You're all to me!
I beg You, hold me closer
than You ever have before;
let Your love be
my soul's lifegiving force.
Accept my feeble effort;
teach me how to love You more;
You are Love and Life itself;
its only Source.

Lord, what wonders You create when You save a wretched soul!
Miracle of miracles! The lost is then made whole!
And there is joy in heaven, such joy we cannot know,
as long as we are locked within these bodies here below.
But someday we will join You and rejoice to see the saving
when one of Your precious children forsakes the world's raving.
What joy - what love divine - when You are all we're craving!
There is no greater miracle than Your love to change a life;
nothing else can cleanse a heart; can empty it of strife.
One touch, one gracious word of love, changes everything!
Hearts that were embattled can drop their guard and fling
all their caution to the winds, and rest within Your arms.
The pain, the hopelessness is gone; they fear not further harms.
The soul that rests secure in You - what troubles can alarm?
Thank You, Gracious Savior; I give my worship and my praise!
You have brought me through this; rejoiced to see me raise
my heart and hands to worship You; You accepted what I gave;
and I know my spirit shall rejoice to see You save
some other mother's baby brought into eternal gladness;
when on earth they knew such grief, such heartrending sadness,
that only You and Your great love has rescued them from madness.
O Christ my Gracious Savior, hold me - hold me tight!
Keep me by Your mercy; lead me in Your light.
Keep me close beside You; I need to feel You near;
let me know Your loving touch; Your sweet voice I must hear.
Keep my heart and spirit centered on You, Beloved King!
I would bring You praise and honor; see Your glory spring
forth to light the universe! My hymns of joy I'll sing.

Thank You, Lord,
I appreciate Your love and grace,
all poured out around me,
making this familiar place
into the mercy seat,
placed before Your throne so grand,
where I kneel before You,
clutching tightly to Your hand.
Only You can help me, Lord;
only You can understand.

Beloved, hear me cry to You;
my heart feels so alone!
I know You have a place for me -
a place I can call home.
I know You've prepared a family,
a fellowship divine;
Lead me, Lord, I beg You,
to this place You say is mine -
I so want to worship you
and see Your glory shine!

My heart, O Lord, I give to Thee,
my soul is Thine as well.
You pour Your love within me,
deeper far than words can tell.
Your peace flows 'round about me,
contentment floods my soul;
Your Holy Spirit's words are sweet;
You wash me and I'm made whole.
I see the smile upon Your face
and hear the music of Your voice.
O help me, Lord, to run this race;
to know the wonder, and rejoice
in knowing that You reign supreme,
Your knowledge and power o'ershade
anything that I could ever dream;
I marvel at the universe You've made!

Jesus, Holy One, before Your throne
I lie with my face to the floor.
My heart and soul I give to You, alone;
My spirit yearns to worship and adore.

Such precious time I spend with You;
in Your Presence I'd happily stay.
Your Spirit cleanses with Your sweet dew;
and Your smile gives joy to my day.

What else can I do but worship You?
Where else would I go, or to whom?
There's only One who is faithful and true;
only One who arose from the tomb!

There's nothing so sweet as to sit at Your feet
while angel choirs sing out Your praise;
I'm but Your sheep, and Your love I entreat;
hear my voice - I rejoice in Your grace!

What love is this, my Lord and King?
What do I see?
I rest against You, so small and weak;
You cuddle me.
You hold me gently to Your breast.
Sweetly, sweetly, milk flows.
It soothes, satisfies and warms.
Never did I think of such a thing -
to be fed from Your own body!
Yes, the bread and wine,
transformed into Your body and blood;
but You insist the image is real.
I accept the sustaining with a cry,
begging for the milk to carry You
into every cell, thought, breath and heartbeat,
until all that I am is infused with You.

Love Beyond All Knowing, King of All Life;
Gracious and Glorious Beyond Imagining;
Glory That Shines Brighter Than All The Suns;
Keeper of My Soul, I bow low before You;
helpless to raise my eyes; to speak Your Name.
I am mute. My heart is ready to burst,
trying to tell You what You already know.

Vainly I've struggled to be "good enough";
endlessly I've asked forgiveness,
but never knew how to accept or receive;
I've wandered through so many years -
years of futility and barrenness;
years of frustration and stagnation;
years of yearning; but now...

You allowed me to see You, and Your love!
In and for another, it is true;
but all the same, it is all the same!
Your love for him is Your love for me -
endlessly deep; heart-stoppingly sweet,
poured out in a crimson Niagara of grace,
blessing all who would seek and ask
and find.

O My child,
you let My words flow through you;
you hear My voice,
and recognize My touch.
Do you still not know?
Each book you read describes things differently;
but it really is as simple as reaching out and taking!
You trusted, and laid your hand in Mine;
I opened your eyes to see,
and you saw
the answer to your years of seeking.
Stand beneath the Niagara, child;
open your heart to the flow.
It is relentless, fierce, pounding.
Flesh cannot remain under its force.
You will be free at last
from all you imagine holds you back -
free to live in and through Me,
as I will live in and through you.

I met You in the garden, where You turned to me;
I heard You say, in loving tones, "Daughter, walk with Me."
The flowers blooming 'round us nodded in assent
as I walked toward You; and my heart was rent
by the sudden sweetness as Your arm encircled me.
I tried to get still closer, even though it couldn't be.
Then, Your arm about my shoulders, and mine around Your waist,
we started off together with what seemed a curious haste.
We scorned the paths between the flowers that we had walked before;
and as we trod upon the flowers, they released their fragrant store,
which drifted up around us, like bubbles of fine scent
as, straight and true, toward the setting sun we went.
The daylight faded quickly and darkness fell apace;
soon I couldn't even see Your beloved face.
And then I could see nothing; but still I felt Your arm
securely heavy on my shoulders, protecting me from harm.
My heart cried out that, Yes, Lord, I would walk with You!
I do not fear the sunset, or whatever I must do.
Just let me feel Your arm, Lord, whenever my heart fails,
and I will seek to do Your will, whatever it entails.

How gracious is Your love for me!
How wondrous is Your care!
Jesus, You are faithful;
there's nothing that could prepare
the yearning, hungry soul
to receive all You want to give;
to feel the power of Your precious grace
granting the will to live.
But always there's a strong desire
to leave this earthly plane;
the struggle to be both here and there
makes me wonder if I'm sane.
My heart desires You wholly; yet,
Lord, I want to do Your will;
as much as I want to be with You,
I will stay here until
You finally let me join You.
Yet, contrarily, You're with me now!
Flowing, whispering, nourishing, sustaining, holding -
Lord, how
can I be in two places at once?
How can You love me so much?
How could I ever doubt Your sweet, sweet words;
Your gentle, loving touch ?

Child, I'm so glad you hear Me
whisper your name;
so glad you accept My sustaining.
So glad you feel My arm and my hand;
so glad you've accepted remaining
until your time on earth is complete,
and I welcome you to Me with joy!
I'm so glad you realize that I'm with you now;
and it's only children who trust I employ
to tell of my love, so others may know
that My love and My grace are for all.
Speak, child; pour out your heart and see
the blessings that I will let fall!

When I cry and You answer;
when I seek and You find;
and all I can do is hold on to You
like one who is blind;
when You tell me to lean
my whole being on You,
and my cares are quieted
and eased when I do;
when Your peace floods my heart,
and spirit and soul,
and I rest in Your arms
while the wee hours roll;
when I feel Your love like a blanket,
so soft and warm,
and around my shoulders
lies the weight of Your arm;
when You grant Your holy Presence
to give me joy to live,
and I feel You urging me
to trust in Your love to give
all that I need to follow You
each moment of each day -
how can I refuse to see
that You won't let me go astray?

Gracious, Glorious King of Kings,
Love Beyond All Knowing,
I feel the depth with which You crave
my loving and my growing.
You know I'll never be my best
'til I seek only You;
and in Your gracious mercy
You know what I must do.
And so You lead me forward
along Your predetermined way,
and keep me so close beside You
that I cannot go astray.
You fill my heart with Your sweet words
of glorious praise
as prayers and tears for others
flow throughout my days.
Thank You, Gracious, Glorious King!
My heart desires You so,
Thank You for placing the desire in me
to learn of You and know
of Your deep love,
so full of goodness, mercy and grace!
Lord, help me seek only You,
Your will and Your face!

Little child, when will you come back?
I miss you!
Hear Me cry from our special place -
you don't come!
I am with you wherever you pray;
but you promised to be alone with Me there,
and I hope each day that you will keep your promise.
Just come, My baby;
I so want to hold you,
love you,
be with you!
O yes; how I want you
fully awakened to My love!
But gently.
Be patient, child:
continue to learn of Me.
Study and read,
there's still much to be internalized;
still much to learn about
worship, adoration and praise.
But first -
return to our place, Beloved!
Come to Me!

Beloved, thank You for hearing my cry;
for Your mercy on me.
You know the loneliness that engulfs me
as I cry for a place where I belong.
Open Your arms and hold me;
give me Yourself,
and I will be content to rest in You.
You tell me to lean back into You,
to rest my whole weight on You,
and You will bear me up.
You tell me
that Your love will never fail;
that the bedrock of the earth,
its very foundations,
will fall apart,
and Your love will still endure.
As I lean back into You,
You tell me to feel Your warmth,
Your heartbeat;
to rest my whole being,
to float on You;
and as Your love envelops me,
my cares drift away on Your tide.

O Gracious Lord, I come to You
and lay my cares and pains at Your feet.
I give them to You; and You shoulder the weight,
and make the burden soft and sweet.

I could not hope to carry it alone;
could not bear the weight of my sin.
But You, O Lord, have taken my load;
have bourne it, and washed me within!

In my daily walk, please yoke me with You;
You promise the load will be light,
for You choose to carry the heaviest part,
and I know You will lead me aright.

Make this walk like a dance, if You will:
grant Your grace through the intricate part;
and I will delight in following Your lead,
for You hold my hand and my heart.

My dear one, why do you marvel?
More seriously, why do you doubt?
You know that I've been doing in you
all you've been reading about.
I know you know the feel of My words
as I slip them into your mind;
you feel the warmth of My passion for you -
the deep love you're starting to find.
You feel the comfort that My arms can give
as I hold you fiercely to Me;
but you laugh at the person who kneels at My throne -
you can't see yourself as I see!
Just for a moment, believe in My love,
and look with the eyes of your soul:
you kneel before Me gowned all in white -
beautiful, radiant, whole.
In My love I see no obvious flaws,
just the heart that seeks only My will;
and the maiden who yearns to know only My love
is blushing, adorable still.
Your outward beauty was fleeting and gone,
but such devotion lends the soul grace.
Look, child, and see how attractive you are
when you want to see only My face!

Beloved, I finally found my place;
but it's not a church my heart sees.
I belong right here in Your throne room,
before Your feet, on my knees!
This is where my heart is filled;
here there is never a drought;
here my heart is verdant and fresh;
here my soul has no doubt.
Here before Your feet, my Love;
here, where Your glory shines;
here, where praise flows unceasingly;
here, where You're truly mine.
Thank You for letting me see myself
bowing low at Your feet;
You've reassured me that I belong,
Your words so gentle and sweet.
I accept with joy the love that You give;
give thanks that You think I'm dear;
accept that I wear a gown of white;
accept the beauty You say that I bear.
I accept Your grace so loving and kind -
accept, though I don't understand;
I never want to leave it now;
help me stay here, holding Your hand.
O, there's only one place where I belong;
I'll strive to see myself there,
kneeling in praise before Your throne,
at the feet of my Love so fair!

I saw myself as a desert,
so barren except for the pain;
and I cried from the depths of my being
for You to send my soul rain.
I saw You as an Oasis,
so lush and beautifully green;
but how small in the vastness of desert
did Your garden seem!
You told me the well was very deep;
my desert could bloom and grow,
if only I'd lift the water
or find a system to guide the flow.
I began to carry the water
and pour bucket loads out on the sand;
and what had been dead began to grow -
greenness covered the land!
I saw great troughs radiating outward
to take the water farther along;
and to praise You for watering my garden,
I lifted my voice in song.
I had feared that I'd soak up all of Your love
and still be empty and bare,
but You showed me I was but a tiny dry dot
in Your Ocean of loving care.
My hunger for love will not destroy You;
You cannot be sullied by sin;
nothing I do can enhance You;
You simply love me, my heart and soul to win.

My child, why do you still feel dry?
How can you resist My flow?
Do you not feel the waves of My Spirit
washing you head to toe?
When you close your eyes, you are floating,
gently rocked by each swell;
I hold you, support you totally,
and reassure you that all will be well.
You know your life's not a desert;
I've provided for your every need;
and you know that, for your garden,
I gave you only the finest of seed.
See how your garden has grown, My love;
see that there is no sand.
Bright flowers bloom, and your tree has grown tall,
all watered by My hand.
Soon your tree will also bloom,
and its fruit will begin to grow;
but first I want you to mature, child,
and to understand, and to know.
As you deepen your prayers and commitment to Me,
I will open to you;
I'll give you insights that you can share,
and show you what you must do.
I told you My ways are not your ways;
My timing is different, too;
but My arms surround you on every side
to keep and to sustain you.

As I knelt to pray that bright sunny day
before Your glorious throne,
You rose from Your seat, raised me to my feet,
said, "Beloved, we are alone.
Come, take the chance; I'll teach you to dance."
And the gown in which I pray
changed from slim and sedate to full and ornate;
from white to silvery grey.
I wish I could say I was graceful that day,
but "clumsy" is too nice a word;
I trampled Your feet, couldn't catch the beat -
not a note of the music I heard!
Your smile stayed in place, Your patience and grace
never showed the effect of the strain;
and after awhile I was able to smile
as I heard You hum the refrain.
I tried to read You and follow Your lead;
O, how I wished I could dance!
And I thank You for taking the time and the pain
required to give me the chance.
I followed You better, though not to the letter;
still, I stepped on You less.
Thank You, my King, for the pleasure You bring -
and for the loan of the dress.

I see myself as I'm deep in prayer
on my knees before Your throne,
when I also see striding up the room
a Roman Centurion.
He walks to where I'm praying
and kneels by my left side -
a warrior is praying with me!
In God's Presence we abide.
And then I notice the colors -
bright gold and brilliant red,
as he reaches to lay a fold of his cloak
over my shoulders and head.
God has called him to strengthen me,
and he has accepted my care!
He - my warrior, my mentor, my guide -
will lead me deeper in prayer.
He is to teach me and guide me;
he'll lend me his strength and his grace;
he'll help me learn to surrender myself,
and choose to seek only Your face!

My warrior once more comes to me
as I'm praying on my knees;
to my left he stands, holds out his hand,
and lifts me to my feet.
Part of me doesn't want to leave
the one place I feel I belong;
it's allowed to stay,
while the rest of me wants to grow and to be strong.
As I go with the warrior I see myself
changed into a warrior as well-
the armor of God replaces my gown of white;
I feel amazement swell!
We step out into bright sunshine,
and the joy of life floods through me -
I don't ever remember feeling such joy -
all bright and new and free!
My spirit dances like a care free child,
and I laugh aloud and sing,
so glad at last to be called to offer
some service to my King!

You gave me wings, Beloved;
You made me a small, white butterfly.
I struggled out of the chrysalis
as I felt my old self finally die.

My new self flew unerringly
to the outstretched finger of a Man,
and I looked and saw so clearly
the nail scars on Your hand.

I flew around Your head in circles,
and as I did, I left a glowing strand;
these strands became a halo,
and then when I wanted to land

Your hand was there for me again,
and You smiled at me as I flew
again and again around Your head
often slipping in close to kiss You.

I'm still flying these haloes,
but bright colors now dot my wings -
reward for loving You, my Lord?
O, You are my everything!

I come to prayer with rushing, whirling thoughts; what a mess!
A hodgepodge of praise and pleas, needs, and much distress.
How to calm my soul? From the depths of the whirlwind came
one coherent thought that lingers, "O, Holy is Your Name!"
The King of Glory comes to me in this moment of silent prayer.
He smiles softly, and I feel the sweetness of His tender care.
How often have I yielded all my heart and soul to Him?
No matter; again I cry, "Take all I am!" And then,
because I can't keep silent, but feel the need to pray,
He lifts me to my feet so we can dance. We gently sway
and just hold each other; no need for words at all,
just peace and calm; and the quiet music fills the hall.
How wonderful! The searching, yearning emptiness is filled!
In gentle swaying, all is understood, and all is stilled.
What do I need? Nothing. What is my heart's cry? Nothing.
Nothing is lacking; nothing is left out; I have Everything.
And the glorious stillness within me - O, praise His holy Name!
What peace is mine; release divine; how glad I am I came!
Freedom from all anxiety, even the prayers that press to be heard
yield to the depths of peace; and there is nothing but the Word.

The rains came, and the winds blew,
and I said, "Lord, where are You?"
The land was flooded, and still it fell;
I said to myself, "This can't be well;
The water will wash away everything!
The destruction's complete; I'll have nothing!"
But in the lull when the storm was done,
I saw the small flowers, one by one,
begin to lift their heads to the sun.
I said, "Lord, the rains were so harsh;
they turned my island into a marsh!
I liked to lie on the hot, dry beach,
and keep the water just out of reach;
to complain of the lack of rain, You see.
Now You've ruined all that for me."
But God said, "Child, you need My rain
to wash away all your guilt and pain.
Look! Your world is all clean again!
Be thankful that you're inundated;
be thankful I water what I created!
I cherish you as your sea walls crumble,
and drench you as you groan and grumble.
It'd be nice to know you appreciated
My efforts to keep your island hydrated.
Again and again I'll sweep over you,
until at long last you're soaked through and through,
and you've learned that I am Faithful and True."

My Lord, would You still send Your poems to me?
Will You open my eyes so I can see,
and put what I see into verse and rhyme?
Will You help me as I wrestle with time
to record what You say, even though I lose sleep -
for mostly I write when the night is deep,
and it's many hours 'til the sun's slow creep.
My heart sings praises to You in the night,
as I finish my prayers and turn out the light.
And when You wake me, I turn to prayer,
and praise Your Name as I'm lying there.
I try to fill my world with thanks to You
for all the problems You've brought me through;
and I praise You for Your love for me, too.
When I praise and honor You, my heart's at ease,
and though the rhyme may not always please,
You love me, and wait for my feeble tries,
as I stop to wipe the sleep from my eyes.
Lord, I'm so glad You want me to pray!
And real worship doesn't just take place by day,
but whenever Your light sends its shining ray.
Once again, Lord, thank You for loving me!
Help me to hear You, and help me to see
Your loving hands at work in my heart and soul.
What joy that You'd pay such a terrible toll
to rescue me from myself and my trial!
Your hand, Your grace, Your wondrous smile-
Lord, any lost sleep is vastly worthwhile!

Most Holy One, my heart seeks you endlessly,
seemingly in vain.
I should have long since realized
all I yearn so to attain.
Should know myself as You see me,
a child of the Great King;
but still I see myself within this world,
and though Your praise I sing,
it's with deep longing for Your love to be fulfilled;
Your joy escapes me.
Hear my cries!
Hear the yearning that fills my being!
Come and see;
show me what must be done,
what is standing in my way!
Surely, all that stands between us is my fault;
I have failed to stay
in Your Presence; failed to attend Thee;
failed....

O, My child, lift up your head!
Lift up your heart!
I've seen the sadness and the tears
even those that died aborning,
your heart too dry even for tears.
I tell you, joy comes in the morning!
Lift up your eyes,
and see your redemption coming!
Even now it is at the gate!
Rejoice!
O, rejoice, My beloved;
I know your yearning.
Behold, I come quickly
to hold you in My arms!
You have not failed to touch Me.
You have not failed to seek
My hand and My face.

My Lord, I lift my hands and my heart;
"Come!" I cry, and I feel the start
of a wing flutter; just a tiny breath
of purity lifts me from my body of death.
I rise, on gossamer wings, into the sky.
My life surrendered, homeward I fly.

O, that my time with You could last!
But it seems mere moments passed,
and I am once more kneeling here,
prayer closet holding me; and a tear
falls silently that I must return
to deal with life; all I can do is yearn.

Thank You, my Lord, for Your tender touch;
thank You for loving me so much
that Your Spirit lifts me for Your smile!
Let me never forget that I'm Your child!.
I praise Your Name as You call me to prayer,
for You will always be with me there.

My child, My arms are open wide;
come lay your head against My side.
Let your tears flow, don't try to hide
the pain you're keeping deep inside.
I know your emptiness, know the pain;
your heart is leaking bitter rain.
Release it all! Let your hurt run free,
as you empty your sorrows onto Me.
My arms hold you fast, you will not fall;
you haven't strayed from My side at all;
be content o stay and whisper your pleas -
I hear you as though you were on your knees.
What do I care of your body's position?
Your heart and soul show your submission.
Yes, I hear you as you praise My Name,
and I promise your life won't stay the same.
We walk into darkness, now, My child,
but you needn't fear the beasts of the wild.
You will be safe, for My path is sure,
and My rod and staff will keep you secure.
So, come, little child, let your sorrows go;
I am your Father; I love you, you know.

Love of My Heart;
Joy of My Soul;
Guardian of My Footsteps,
I yearn for You!
By myself I can do nothing.
You give me breath
and set the rhythm of my heartbeats.
You breathe Your music through my soul
and Your fragrance lingers
to entice me back,
again and again,
to find the echo of Your aroma,
and perhaps catch a fleeting glimpse of you
to dazzle my heart.
Come! O, come, Beloved!
Let Your love envelop me once again!
Hold me in Your arms;
I can only adore You,
and seek to draw closer -
ever closer!